An aid to The Call:

A Pastor's Guidebook for preparing the ministerial candidate.

By Lawrence E Smith Jr

Edited by Pastor Scott Thomas

With contributions from Pastor Emeritus Jesse Frazier & Pastor Scott Thomas

First Edition

ISBN: 979-8-218-80931-7

GODisBIG Publishing

About the Guidebook

The purpose of this guidebook is to give the pastor a bit of a foundational structure to assist those who have responded to their call to the ministry. It should not be used to determine if God has called someone. Only God can do that. My suggestion would be to acknowledge the call and help the pastor assist and train the ministerial candidate and make a better determination of the fit of the candidate in the local assembly.

Ideally, the guidebook will confirm the candidate's strengths while aiding in reinforcing areas that are more challenging. Also, things like pulpit etiquette, tithing as a mandate, or behavior while visiting another church are left to the pastor to govern, so they are not addressed here.

If the pastor is thorough, it could take some time to navigate through the guidebook. Ideally, the minister candidate is probably, in some compacity, already availing themselves of some aspects of ministry or leadership, so time should not be a consideration for completion of the evaluation. There will be several editions of the book as areas and sections are tweaked and others' added based on feedback from ministers and pastors. It is my prayer that this will be of help in both the pastor and the ministerial candidate confirm their role in the body of Christ so that God will get the glory and honor in everything.

Grace & Peace

Acknowledgements & Dedications

The Triune Godhead – How can I not acknowledge the One to whom I owe my existence? God loved me by giving of His Son for my transgression, and then indwelt me with His Holy Spirit to come along side me as I stumble and bumble through this life. I am so grateful for His mercy, grace, and lovingkindness. If I were equipped with every available word that ever existed in all available languages, I would never be able to fully express my thankfulness, even if given an eternity to do so.

Treva Smith – Treva is the personification of God's blessing to me. If He never does anything else, I am satisfied with His gift of Himself and His gift of Treva to me. As of this writing, she has suffered as my wife for over 27 years, and I love her so much more than I did on day one. I am not only praying for at least another 27 years, but for a home next to hers when we go to heaven.

Jesse & Shirley Frazier, Rosie Roberson – With every completed effort I will always talk about these three. Each of them has been instrumental in my upbringing in one way or another and I will always be appreciative to God for placing them in my life. I could not be who I am without these three.

Pastor Jerome Tolliver - This book was borne out of a conversation we had while in Branson, MO. I thank God for your heart and the interactions we have had over the years. I love you and I am grateful for our friendship.

I would also like to acknowledge **Jesse Frazier** & **Scott Thomas** for not only contributing to this work but for giving valuable advice and information in its creation. Thank you so much for opening up your hearts and giving of your time.

Identifying the Call

Those who have received the calling of a minister should also be exhibiting the marks of a mature believer. That evidence should be manifested in the candidate's life according to Scripture as well as confirmed by witnesses. Candidates should display the fruit of the Spirit according to Galatians 5:22-23, be a pursuer of what God has called him to do according to Philippians 3:12-16, and should continue to be diligent in their call according to 2 Peter 1:5-8.

In the following pages, there is a spiritual gift assessment that can be used to determine what type of ministry the candidate can be placed in to be most effective. This will certainly not only benefit the church, but also the individual because he will not only be vested, but will also be fulfilled in the work. The assessments consist of various statements in which the candidate would simply place the numbers 1 through 5 next to it, 1 meaning the statement is not absolutely true about them through 5 being absolutely true. The assessments have three statements geared to help determine a partiality to each gift. There are two types of assessments attached. The regular assessment the candidate takes will not have the name of the gifts to encourage an honest evaluation of themselves. The assessment for leaders should be used to add up the answers and determine where the candidate's gifting is strongest.

There is also a Ministerial Candidate Assessment that has two parts. The first part is an observational evaluation of traits based on 1 Timothy 3 & Titus 1. The pastor (and committee, if one is appointed) rate each trait from 1 (does not demonstrate) to 5 (Consistently demonstrates). The rest of the evaluation can be conducted as either written or interview questions after which, based on the answers, the pastor or committee score based on the evaluation criteria. Each set of questions are meant to determine things like Biblical Competency, Emotional Intelligence, Leadership Capability, and Empathy and Pastoral Sensitivity. Again, there is an assessment for the candidate and one for those who are doing the evaluation. Based on the Summary Evaluation, you may choose to not go forward with Ministerial Development. This does not determine the call, but simply means the candidate may not be ready at the time. The pastor, who should have insight on the candidate, should always have the final word in this manner.

Others in the church should also be able to confirm the marks of the mature believer as he operates in the local church. Some of the other things the pastor may require of the minister is active giving, attendance of services and church meetings regularly, and being available for other things as they come up.

Potential Gift Assessment

Detailed Spiritual Gift Assessment Questionnaire

Instructions:

- **Read each statement carefully.**

- **Rate how true the statement is for you using the following scale:**

Rating Meaning

1   **Rarely true**

2   **Occasionally true**

3   **Sometimes true**

4   **Often true**

5   **Consistently or very true**

---

1. **I enjoy organizing people and tasks to accomplish goals.**

2. I can see the big picture and plan steps to reach it.

3. Others follow my lead in group settings.

4. I prefer working behind the scenes to assist others.

5. I willingly do small or unnoticed tasks.

6. I feel joy in making others successful.

7. I enjoy researching and explaining biblical truths.

8. I prepare carefully when I teach or lead discussions.

9. People say I help them understand God's Word more clearly.

10. I often feel called to speak hope into others' lives.

11. People seek me out when they need motivation or comfort.

12. I naturally challenge others to grow spiritually.

13. I give generously even when it's sacrificial.

14. I'm joyful when I can meet someone's needs financially or materially.

15. I budget to make room for giving.

16. I can often sense spiritual deception before others.

17. I rely on inner conviction and Scripture when making judgments.

18. People ask me for advice when they are unsure about spiritual matters.

19. I'm drawn to help the suffering or the lonely.

20. I feel deep empathy for those in pain.

21. I avoid judging others and try to understand them first.

22. I have moments of insight that prove spiritually accurate.

23. I often see connections in Scripture others overlook.

24. People are surprised by what I know or discern spiritually.

25. I often see solutions to spiritual or life problems.

26. Others ask for my advice in tough situations.

27. My counsel aligns with God's Word and brings peace.

28. I believe God will act even when circumstances say otherwise.

29. I trust God deeply in uncertainty or trials.

30. People have called my faith "strong" or "inspiring."

31. I have prayed for people to be healed and saw results.

32. I sense God prompting me to pray for healing.

33. I believe God still heals physically, emotionally, and spiritually.

34. I have witnessed or experienced supernatural acts of God.

35. I believe God works powerfully through faith and prayer.

36. I pray expecting God to do the impossible.

37. I have spoken or prayed in a spiritual language unknown to me.

38. Tongues strengthen my personal connection to God.

39. I believe tongues are a gift meant to edify the Church.

40. I have understood or interpreted a spiritual language.

41. I have felt led to share what I believe God was saying in tongues.

42. Interpretation brings clarity and peace to others.

43. I feel burdened for those who don't know Jesus.

44. I easily share the gospel in conversation.

45. I've led someone to faith in Christ.

46. I care deeply for the spiritual well-being of others.

47. People come to me for spiritual direction or prayer.

48. I enjoy mentoring or discipling others in their walk with Christ.

49. I enjoy welcoming guests into my home or group.

50. I go out of my way to make others feel included.

51. I create environments where people feel safe and valued.

52. I feel a strong desire to proclaim biblical truth boldly.

53. I sense when God has a word for someone or the church.

54. I speak out even when it's uncomfortable, if God leads.

55. I'm drawn to start new ministries or churches.

56. I see spiritual opportunities in uncharted areas.

57. Others follow my vision for expanding God's kingdom.

58. I feel burdened to pray for others, often for long periods.

59. I've seen God move in response to specific prayers.

60. I feel energized and connected to God during deep prayer.

List other skills or talents that may be beneficial for your local church body.

- Reflect:
    - Have others affirmed these in me?
    - Am I using them in service today?
    - Do I want to develop them further?

Potential Gift Assessment – For Leaders

Detailed Spiritual Gift Assessment Questionnaire

Instructions:

- Read each statement carefully.

- Rate how true the statement is for you using the following scale:

Rating Meaning

1   Rarely true

2   Occasionally true

3   Sometimes true

4   Often true

5   Consistently or very true

Administration/Leadership (Rom. 12:8, 1 Cor. 12:28)

1. I enjoy organizing people and tasks to accomplish goals.

2. I can see the big picture and plan steps to reach it.

3. Others follow my lead in group settings.

4. I enjoy organizing people and tasks to accomplish goals.

5. I can see the big picture and plan steps to reach it.

6. Others follow my lead in group settings.

Helps/Service (1 Cor. 12:28, Rom. 12:7)

7. I prefer working behind the scenes to assist others.

8. I willingly do small or unnoticed tasks.

9. I feel joy in making others successful.

Teaching (Rom. 12:7, 1Cor. 12:28)

10. I enjoy researching and explaining biblical truths.

11. I prepare carefully when I teach or lead a discussion.

12. People say I help them understand God's Word more clearly.

Exhortation/Encouragement (Rom. 12:8)

13. I often feel called to speak hope into others' lives.

14. People seek me out when they need motivation or comfort.

15. I naturally challenge others to grow spiritually.

Giving (Rom. 12:8)

16. I give generously even when it's sacrificial.

17. I'm joyful when I can meet someone's need financially or materially.

18. I budget to make room for giving.

Discernment (1 Cor. 12:10)

19. I can often sense spiritual deception before others.

20. I rely on inner conviction and Scripture when making judgments.

21. People ask me for advice when unsure about spiritual matters.

Mercy (Rom. 12:8)

22. I'm drawn to help the suffering or lonely.

23. I feel deep empathy for those in pain.

24. I avoid judging others and try to understand them first.

Word of Knowledge (1 Cor. 12:8)

25. I have moments of insight that prove spiritually accurate.

26. I often see connections in Scripture others overlook.

27. People are surprised by what I know or discern spiritually.

Word of Wisdom (1 Cor. 12:8)

28. I often see solutions to spiritual or life problems.

29. Others ask for my advice in tough situations.

30. My counsel aligns with God's Word and brings peace.

Faith (1 Cor. 12:9)

31. I believe God will act even when circumstances say otherwise.

32. I trust God deeply in uncertainty or trials.

33. People have called my faith "strong" or "inspiring."

Healing (1 Cor. 12:9)

34. I have prayed for people to be healed and seen results.

35. I sense God prompting me to pray for healing.

36. I believe God still heals physically, emotionally, and spiritually.

Miracles (1 Cor. 12:10)

37. I have witnessed or experienced supernatural acts of God.

38. I believe God works powerfully through faith and prayer.

39. I pray expecting God to do the impossible.

Tongues (1 Cor. 12:10)

40. I have spoken or prayed in a spiritual language unknown to me.

41. Tongues strengthen my personal connection to God.

42. I believe tongues are a gift meant to edify the Church.

Interpretation of Tongues (1 Cor. 12:10)

43. I have understood or interpreted a spiritual language.

44. I have felt led to share what I believe God was saying in tongues.

45. Interpretation brings clarity and peace to others.

Evangelism (Eph. 4:11)

46. I feel burdened for those who don't know Jesus.

47. I easily share the gospel in conversation.

48. I've led someone to faith in Christ.

Shepherding/Pastoring (Eph. 4:11)

49. I care deeply for the spiritual well-being of others.

50. People come to me for spiritual direction or prayer.

51. I enjoy mentoring or discipling others in their walk with Christ.

Hospitality (1 Pet. 4:9-10)

52. I enjoy welcoming guests into my home or group.

53. I go out of my way to make others feel included.

54. I create environments where people feel safe and valued.

Prophecy (Rom. 12:6, 1 Cor. 12:10)

55. I feel a strong desire to proclaim biblical truth boldly.

56. I sense when God has a word for someone or the church.

57. I speak out even when it's uncomfortable, if God leads.

Apostleship (Eph. 4:11, 1 Cor. 12:28)

58. I'm drawn to start new ministries or churches.

59. I see spiritual opportunities in uncharted areas.

60. Others follow my vision for expanding God's kingdom.

Intercession (Implied in 1 Tim. 2:1, Rom. 8:26)

61. I feel burdened to pray for others, often for long periods.

62. I've seen God move in response to specific prayers.

63. I feel energized and connected to God during deep prayer.

⏹ Scoring Guide

Step 1: Tally Your Scores

- Group questions in sets of 3 per gift.
- Add the scores for each group (3–15 range per gift).

Gift	Question Numbers	Total Score
Administration	1–3	___
Helps	4–6	___
Teaching	7–9	___
Encouragement	10–12	___
Giving	13–15	___
Discernment	16–18	___
Mercy	19–21	___
Knowledge	22–24	___
Wisdom	25–27	___
Faith	28–30	___

Gift	Question Numbers	Total Score
Healing	31–33	___
Miracles	34–36	___
Tongues	37–39	___
Interpretation	40–42	___
Evangelism	43–45	___
Shepherding	46–48	___
Hospitality	49–51	___
Prophecy	52–54	___
Apostleship	55–57	___
Intercession	58–60	___

Step 2: Interpret Your Results

Step 3: Next Steps

- **Highlight your top 3–5 gifts.**
- **Reflect:**

- Have others affirmed these in the candidate?

- Is the candidate using them in service today?

- Do you want to develop them further?

Potential Initial Ministerial Candidate Assessment

"Not a recent convert... but must be well thought of by outsiders..." – 1 Timothy 3:6–7 "Entrust to reliable people who will also be qualified to teach others." – 2 Timothy 2:2

I. Foundational Biblical Qualifications (Based on 1 Timothy 3 & Titus 1)

Assess the candidate on these **core biblical character traits**. Rate each from 1 (Does not demonstrate) to 5 (Strongly demonstrates):

Trait	Scriptural Basis	Rating (1–5)	Comments
Above reproach	1 Tim 3:2	___	
Faithful in marriage	1 Tim 3:2	___	
Self-controlled	Titus 1:8	___	
Respectable	1 Tim 3:2	___	
Hospitable	1 Tim 3:2	___	

Trait	Scriptural Basis	Rating (1–5)	Comments
Able to teach	1 Tim 3:2	____	
Not violent but gentle	1 Tim 3:3	____	
Not quarrelsome	1 Tim 3:3	____	
Not a lover of money	1 Tim 3:3	____	
Manages household well	1 Tim 3:4	____	
Not a recent convert	1 Tim 3:6	____	
Has a good reputation with outsiders	1 Tim 3:7	____	

📖 II.

Written or Interview Questions:

1. How do you explain the gospel in one minute?

2. Describe your understanding of the Trinity using Scripture.

3. What do you believe about the authority and inspiration of the Bible?

4. How do you prepare a sermon or Bible study? (Walk through your process.)

5. How would you explain Romans 8:28 to someone who just experienced a tragedy?

6. How do you differentiate between cultural interpretation and timeless truth in Scripture?

7. What role does the Holy Spirit play in the life of a believer?

Evaluation Criteria (1–5):

- Theological accuracy

- Scripture-based responses

- Ability to communicate clearly to both believers and seekers.

☐ III.

Interview Questions:

1. Describe a time when you were criticized. How did you respond?

2. What emotions do you struggle with most, and how do you manage them?

3. How do you manage conflict within a team or church body?

4. How do you maintain humility in leadership?

5. Tell me about a time you misunderstood someone. What did you learn?

Rating Categories (1–5):

Competency	Description	Rating
Self-awareness	Understands personal triggers, limits	——
Self-regulation	Manages stress, conflict, emotion appropriately	——
Social awareness	Picks up on others' emotions and needs	——
Relational management	Manages tough conversations with grace	——

☐ IV.

Interview Questions:

1. Share a time you led a team or ministry. What was your role?

2. How do you cast vision and keep people engaged?

3. What do you do when people resist your leadership or direction?

4. Describe a time you failed in leadership and what you learned.

5. How do you balance delegation with accountability?

Leadership Evaluation (1–5):

Area	Indicators	Rating
Vision casting	Inspires and aligns others around a mission	——
Organization	Plans, delegates, and executes effectively	——
Conflict navigation	Resolves disputes with wisdom and grace	——
Team-building	Draws out and develops others' gifts	——

♥ **V.**

Interview Questions:

1. Describe a time you walked with someone through grief or trauma.

2. How do you balance truth and compassion when counseling someone in sin?

3. What does it mean to be present with someone in their pain?

4. How would you approach a church member who is withdrawing from community?

5. How do you guard against burnout while still being available to people?

Rating Categories (1–5):

Skill	Description	Rating
Listening	Attentive and non-judgmental presence	____
Compassion	Feels with and for others	____
Discernment	Knows when to speak, pray, or just sit	____
Boundaries	Maintains availability without overload	____

VI.

Questions:

1. Describe your daily devotional practices.

2. What has God been teaching you recently?

3. How do you stay spiritually refreshed during dry seasons?

4. Who disciples you or holds you accountable?

5. What spiritual disciplines shape your walk with Christ?

Rating Criteria (1–5):

- Consistence in personal devotion

- Openness to accountability

- Clear evidence of a Spirit-led life

📜 Summary Evaluation Page

Area	Average Score	Comments
Biblical Qualifications	___	
Biblical Competency	___	
Emotional Intelligence	___	
Leadership Capability	___	
Empathy / Pastoral Care	___	
Spiritual Maturity	___	

Overall Recommendation:

- Strongly Recommend

- Recommend with Development Plan

- Not Ready at This Time

Potential Initial Ministerial Candidate Assessment for Leaders

"Not a recent convert... but must be well thought of by outsiders..." – 1 Timothy 3:6–7 "Entrust to reliable people who will also be qualified to teach others." – 2 Timothy 2:2

I. Foundational Biblical Qualifications (Based on 1 Timothy 3 & Titus 1)

Assess the candidate on these **core biblical character traits**. Rate each from 1 (Does not demonstrate) to 5 (Strongly demonstrates):

Trait	Scriptural Basis	Rating (1–5)	Comments
Above reproach	1 Tim 3:2	___	
Faithful in marriage	1 Tim 3:2	___	
Self-controlled	Titus 1:8	___	
Respectable	1 Tim 3:2	___	
Hospitable	1 Tim 3:2	___	

43

Trait	Scriptural Basis	Rating (1–5)	Comments
Able to teach	1 Tim 3:2	___	
Not violent but gentle	1 Tim 3:3	___	
Not quarrelsome	1 Tim 3:3	___	
Not a lover of money	1 Tim 3:3	___	
Manages household well	1 Tim 3:4	___	
Not a recent convert	1 Tim 3:6	___	
Has a good reputation with outsiders	1 Tim 3:7	___	

📖 II. Biblical Competency

These questions assess the candidate's **doctrinal soundness** and ability to interpret Scripture with clarity and faithfulness.

Written or Interview Questions:

8. How do you explain the gospel in one minute?

9. Describe your understanding of the Trinity using Scripture.

10. What do you believe about the authority and inspiration of the Bible?

11. How do you prepare a sermon or Bible study? (Walk through your process.)

12. How would you explain Romans 8:28 to someone who just experienced a tragedy?

13. How do you differentiate between cultural interpretation and timeless truth in Scripture?

14. What role does the Holy Spirit play in the life of a believer?

Evaluation Criteria (1–5):

- Theological accuracy
- Scripture-based responses
- Ability to communicate clearly to both believers and seekers

---

☐ **III. Emotional Intelligence (EQ)**

These questions help assess the candidate's **self-awareness, relational maturity, and emotional regulation**.

Interview Questions:

6. Describe a time when you were criticized. How did you respond?

7. What emotions do you struggle with most, and how do you manage them?

8. How do you manage conflict within a team or church body?

9. How do you maintain humility in leadership?

10. Tell me about a time you misunderstood someone. What did you learn?

Rating Categories (1–5):

Competency	Description	Rating
Self-awareness	Understands personal triggers, limits	——
Self-regulation	Manages stress, conflict, emotion appropriately	——
Social awareness	Picks up on others' emotions and needs	——
Relational management	Manages tough conversations with grace	——

☐ IV. Basic Leadership Capability

Evaluates the candidate's potential to **organize, influence, and guide others** in a ministry context.

Interview Questions:

6. Share a time you led a team or ministry. What was your role?

7. How do you cast vision and keep people engaged?

8. What do you do when people resist your leadership or direction?

9. Describe a time you failed in leadership and what you learned.

10. How do you balance delegation with accountability?

Leadership Evaluation (1–5):

Area	Indicators	Rating
Vision casting	Inspires and aligns others around a mission	——
Organization	Plans, delegates, and executes effectively	——
Conflict navigation	Resolves disputes with wisdom and grace	——
Team-building	Draws out and develops others' gifts	——

♥ V. Empathy and Pastoral Sensitivity

Measures how well the candidate relates to the emotional and spiritual needs of others.

Interview Questions:

6. Describe a time you walked with someone through grief or trauma.

7. How do you balance truth and compassion when counseling someone in sin?

8. What does it mean to be present with someone in their pain?

9. How would you approach a church member who is withdrawing from community?

10. How do you guard against burnout while still being available to people?

Rating Categories (1–5):

Skill	Description	Rating
Listening	Attentive and non-judgmental presence	——
Compassion	Feels with and for others	——
Discernment	Knows when to speak, pray, or just sit	——
Boundaries	Maintains availability without overload	——

VI. Spiritual Maturity and Devotion

Questions:

6. Describe your daily devotional practices.

7. What has God been teaching you recently?

8. How do you stay spiritually refreshed during dry seasons?

9. Who disciples you or holds you accountable?

10. What spiritual disciplines shape your walk with Christ?

Rating Criteria (1–5):

- Consistence in personal devotion
- Openness to accountability
- Clear evidence of a Spirit-led life

🏛 Summary Evaluation Page

Area	Average Score	Comments
Biblical Qualifications	___	
Biblical Competency	___	
Emotional Intelligence	___	
Leadership Capability	___	
Empathy / Pastoral Care	___	
Spiritual Maturity	___	

Overall Recommendation:

- Strongly Recommend

- Recommend with Development Plan

- Not Ready at This Time

Tiered Training

It would be imprudent to think all ministerial candidates enter the call with the same level of knowledge and maturity. The following pages are designed to allow the pastor to develop the candidate based on their experience in ministry. What I would consider as Tier I is a level at which a great deal of knowledge or education has to be passed on to the candidate to maximize their effectiveness of service within the church body. This would include things like basic Biblical Interpretation, information regarding Systematic Theology and Doctrinal Essentials. Tier II would lean toward things such as Ministry Skills Development, Preaching and Teaching, Membership Care, and Evangelism.

Please keep in mind some of the subject matter could be taught on several levels, and that learning should take place for the rest of our lives. The information is placed in tiers to help the pastor determine what areas can be prioritized regarding their candidate. Upper Tiers will have less information but will concentrate on sources that can be relied on to take training or experience beyond what we are able to do in this book.

It is also important to keep in mind that any direction taken should be tailored for the benefit of your local church body and its surrounding community. Some pastors consider an extensive knowledge of the Church Covenant essential in training even though it's not mentioned here. This book is not considered comprehensive in its coverage, but offers that which would be deemed helpful in the training and development of the ministerial candidates. As always, the pages can be changed or tweaked by the pastor based on the local needs of the church.

Tier I – Doctrinal Essentials[1]

Rupertus Meldenius, a Lutheran theologian and educator has been credited for the quote "In essentials, unity; in nonessentials, liberty; in all things, charity." There should be an agreement among those in the Christian faith regarding the following doctrinal essentials. Any disagreement of the following should be examined carefully in light of Scripture in its proper context.

The resurrection of Christ – Christ's resurrection is one of the essentials, if not *the* essential, because it is so basic to the Christian faith. Without the resurrection of Christ, we are without hope for eternal life. "If Christ has not been raised, our preaching is useless and so is your faith" (1 Corinthians 15:14). With His resurrection, Christ proved that He had made a satisfactory payment for sin, that His victory over sin and death was literal and complete, and that He has the power to save.

The gospel – The message of the gospel, or good news, is that Jesus died for sinner and rose again the third day. Paul spells this out in 1 Corinthians

---

[1] "What are the essentials of the Christian Faith?", n.p., https://www.gotquestions.org/essentials-Christian-faith.htm

15:1-4. Paul also warns against false gospels that replace Christ's work with our own or in some other way lead the unsuspecting away from the cross and empty tomb. The pure gospel of Jesus Christ – His death on the cross and His resurrection to everlasting life – is an essential of the Christian faith. More than that, "it is the power of God that brings salvation to everyone who believes" (Romans 1:16).

The deity of Christ – Quite simply, Jesus is God. While Jesus never directly says, "I am God" in Scripture, He makes it clear that He is God in the flesh. Jesus taught, "I and the Father are one" (John 10:30), and in this way He claimed deity. On occasions when people called Him "God," Jesus does not deny it. An example is John 20:28, when Thomas addresses Jesus as "My Lord and my God!" Jesus accepts the title because it is an accurate description of who He is. His resurrection from the dead is one of the main proofs of His deity.

Salvation by grace – We are all sinners separated from God and deserving of eternal punishment for our sin. Jesus' death on the cross paid for the sins of mankind – the just died for the unjust (1 Peter 3:18). Because of Jesus' sacrifice on our behalf, we can be forgiven and have an eternal relationship with God. God did not have to do this for us-we were unworthy of such love – but He sent His only Son as an act of grace, or underserved favor. Scripture emphasizes the goodness and grace of God: "For it is by grace you have been saved, through faith – and this is not from yourselves, it is the gift of God- not by works, so that no one can boast" (Ephesians 2:8-9. There is nothing we can do to earn God's favor or gain access to heaven. Salvation is all of grace.

Salvation through Jesus Christ alone – Some people wonder, "Don't all roads lead to God?" At least in one sense, all roads *do* lead to God – everyone will face Him in judgment after death. But not everyone will be saved. For most people, the judgment will be a terrible occasion, as they will not know Jesus as their Lord. Those who do not have faith in Christ will have the lake of fire as their final destination. There is only way to avoid that fate: faith in god's Son, Jesus Christ. Jesus is the only Savior: "Salvation is found in no one else, for there is no other name under heaven given to mankind by which we must be saved" (Acts 4:12). Jesus' sacrifice on the cross is our only remedy for sin. His resurrection is our only hope for eternal life. Jesus' own words on the matter are quite exclusive: "I am the way, the truth, and the life. No one comes to the Father except through me" (John 14:6).

Monotheism – Monotheism is the belief that there is only one god to be worshiped and served, and that belief is an essential of the Christian faith. Monotheism is taught throughout Scripture, starting with the law and continuing through the prophets: "This is what the Lord says – Israel's King and Redeemer, the LORD Almighty; I am the first and I am the last; apart from Me there is no God" (Isaiah 44:6). The New Testament affirms the same truth, and a Christian knows there is only one true God, despite the many wannabes.

The holy Trinity – A doctrine basic to Christianity is that god the Father, God the Son, and God the Holy Spirit are all the one God. The concept of a "three-in-one" God is not taught in a single verse or passage, but Scripture repeatedly alludes to His triune nature. In Matthew 28:19, all three Persons of the Trinity are mentioned. "There go and make disciples of all nations, baptizing them in the name of the Father and of the Son and of the Holy Spirit." All three Persons of the Trinity are also present at Jesus' baptism (Matthew 3:17). Christians may not be able to adequately explain the Trinity, but they believe that God is triune.

Tier I – Articles of Faith

Articles of faith are the summary statements of foundational beliefs held by individuals, churches, or ministries. They set forth the essential truth which guides every area of belief and practice. The following are the Articles of Faith for a traditional church that believes in the grammatical-historical tradition of interpreting Scripture.

I. OF THE SCRIPTURES

We believe that the Holy Bible was written by men divinely inspired, and is a perfect treasure of heavenly instruction; that it has God for its author, salvation for its end, and truth without any mixture of error for its matter; that it reveals the principles by which God will judge us; and therefore is, and shall remain to the end of the world, the true center of Christian union, and the supreme standard by which all human conduct, creeds, and opinions should be tried.

1. 2 Tim. 3:16-17; 2 Pet. 1:21; 1 Sam. 23:2; Acts 1:16; 3:21; John 10:35; Luke 16:29-31; Psa. 119:11; Rom. 3:1-2

2. 2 Tim. 3:15; 1 Pet. 1:10-12; Acts 11:14; Rom. 1:16; Mark 16:16; John 5:38-39.

3. Prov. 30:5-6; John 17:17; Rev. 22:18-19; Rom. 3:4.

4. Rom. 2:12; John 12:47-48; 1 Cor. 4:3-4; Luke 10:10-16; 12:47-48.

5. Phil. 3:16; Eph. 4:3-6; Phil. 2:1-2; 1 Cor. 1:10; 1 Pet. 4:11.

6. 1 John 4:1; Isa. 8:20; 1 Thess. 5:21; 2 Cor. 8:5; Acts 17:11; 1 John 4:6; Jude 3:5; Eph. 6:17; Psa. 119:59-60; Phil. 1:9-11.

II. OF THE TRUE GOD

We believe that there is one, and only one, living and true God, an infinite, intelligent Spirit, whose name is JEHOVAH, the Maker and Supreme Ruler of Heaven and earth; inexpressibly glorious in holiness, and worthy of all possible honor, confidence, and love; that in the unity of the Godhead there are three persons, the Father, the Son, and the Holy Ghost; equal in every divine perfection, and executing distinct and harmonious offices in the great work of redemption.

1. John 4:24; Psa. 147:5; 83:18; Heb. 3:4; Rom. 1:20; Jer. 10:10

2. Exod. 15:11; Isa. 6:3; 1 Pet. 1:15-16; Rev. 4:6-8

3. Mark 12:30; Rev. 4:11; Matt. 10:37; Jer. 2:12-13

4. Matt. 28:19; John 15:26; 1 Cor. 12:4-6; 1 John 5:7

5. John 10:30; 5:17; 14:23; 17:5, 10; Acts 5:3-4; 1 Cor. 2:10-11; Phil. 2:5-6

6. Eph. 2:18; 2 Cor. 13:14; Rev. 1:4-5; comp. 2, 7

III. OF THE FALL OF MAN

We believe that man was created in holiness, under the law of his Maker; but by voluntary transgression fell from that holy and happy state; in consequence of which all mankind are now sinners, not by constraint, but choice; being by nature utterly void of that holiness required by the law of God, positively inclined to evil; and therefore under just condemnation to eternal ruin, without defense or excuse.

1. Gen. 1:27, 31; Eccl. 7:29; Acts 16:26; Gen. 2:16

2. Gen. 3:6-24; Rom. 5:12

3. Rom. 5:19; John 3:6; Psa. 51:5; Rom. 5:15-19; 8:7

4. Isa. 53:6; Gen. 6:12; Rom. 3:9-18

5. Eph. 2:1-3; Rom. 1:18, 32; 2:1-16; Gal. 3:10; Matt. 20:15

6. Ezek. 18:19-20; Rom. 1:20; 3:19; Gal. 3:22

IV. OF THE WAY OF SALVATION

We believe that the salvation of sinners is wholly of grace, through the mediatorial offices of the Son of God; who by the appointment of the Father, freely took upon him our nature, yet without sin; honored the divine law by his personal obedience, and by his death made a full atonement for our sins; that having risen from the death, he is now enthroned in heaven; and uniting in his wonderful person the tenderest sympathies with divine perfections, he is every way qualified to be a suitable, a compassionate, and an all- sufficient Savior.

1. Eph. 2:5; Matt. 18:11; 1 John 4:10; 1 Cor. 3:5-7; Acts 15:11

2. John 3:16; 1:1-14; Heb. 4:14; 12:24

3. Phil. 2:6-7; Heb. 2:9, 14; 2 Cor. 5:21

4. Isa. 42:21; Phil. 2:8; Gal. 4:4-5; Rom. 3:21

5. Isa. 53:4-5; Matt. 20:28; Rom. 4:25; 3:21-26; 1 John 4:10.

6. 2:2; 1 Cor. 15:1-3; Heb. 9:13-15

7. Heb. 1:8, 3; 8:1; Col. 3:1-4

8. Heb. 7:25; Col. 2:9; Heb. 2:18; 7:26; Psa. 89:19; Psa. 14

V. OF JUSTIFICATION

We believe that the great gospel blessing which Christ secures to such as believe in him is Justification; that Justification includes the pardon of sin, and the promise of eternal life on principles of righteousness; that it is bestowed, not in consideration of any works of righteousness which we have done, but solely through faith in the Redeemer's blood; by virtue of which faith his perfect righteousness is freely imputed to us of God; that it brings us into a state of most blessed peace and favor with God, and secures every other blessing needful for time and eternity.

1. John 1:16; Eph. 3:8

2. Acts 13:39; Isa. 3:11-12; Rom. 8:1

3. Rom. 5:9; Zech. 13:1; Matt. 9:6; Acts 10:43

4. Rom. 5:17; Titus 3:5-6; 1 Pet. 3:7; 1 John 2:25; Rom. 5:21

5. Rom. 4:4-5; 5:21; 6:28; Phil. 3:7-9

6. Rom. 5:19; 3:24-26; 4:23-25; 1 John 2:12

VI. OF THE FREENESS OF SALVATION

We believe that the blessings of salvation are made free to all by the gospel; that it is the immediate duty of all to accept them by a cordial, penitent, and obedient faith; and that nothing prevents the salvation of the greatest sinner on earth but his own inherent depravity and voluntary rejection of the gospel; which rejection involves him in an aggravated condemnation.

1. Isa. 55:1; Rev. 22:17; Luke 14:17

2. Rom. 16:26; Mark 1:15; Rom. 1:15-17

3. John 5:40; Matt. 23:37; Rom. 9:32; Prov. 1:24; Acts 13:46

4. John 3:19; Matt. 11:20; Luke 19:27; 2 Thess. 1:8

VII. OF GRACE IN REGENERATION

We believe that, in order to be saved, sinners must be regenerated, or born again; that regeneration consists in giving a holy disposition to the mind; that it is effected in a manner above our comprehension by the power of the Holy Spirit, in connection with divine truth, so as to secure our voluntary obedience to the gospel; and that its proper evidence appears in the holy fruits of repentance, and faith, and newness of life.

1. John 3:3, 6-7; 1 Cor. 1:14; Rev. 8:7-9; 21:27

2. 2 Cor. 5:17; Ezek. 36:26; Deut. 30:6; Rom. 2:28-29; 5:5; 1 John 4:7

3. John 3:8; 1:13; James 1:16-18; 1 Cor. 1:30; Phil. 2:13

4. 1 Pet. 1:22-25; 1 John 5:1; Eph. 4:20-24; Col. 3:9-11

5. Eph. 5:9; Rom. 8:9; Gal. 5:16-23; Eph. 3:14-21; Matt. 3:8-10; 7:20; 1 John 5:4, 18

VIII. OF REPENTANCE AND FAITH

We believe that Repentance and Faith are sacred duties, and also inseparable graces, wrought in our souls by the regenerating Spirit of God; whereby being deeply convinced of our guilt, danger, and helplessness, and of the way of salvation by Christ, we turn to God with unfeigned contrition, confession, and supplication for mercy; at the same time heartily receiving the Lord Jesus Christ as our Prophet, Priest, and King, and relying on him alone as the only and all-sufficient Savior.

1. Mark 1:15; Acts 11:18; Eph. 2:8; 1 John 5:1

2. John 16:8; Acts 2:37-38; 16:30-31

3. Luke 18:13; 15:18-21; James 4:7-10; 2 Cor. 7:11; Rom.10:12-13; Psa. 51

4. Rom. 10:9-11; Acts 3:22-23: Heb. 4:14; Psa. 2:6; Heb. 1:8; 8:25; 2 Tim. 1:12

IX. OF GOD'S PURPOSE OF GRACE

We believe that Election is the eternal purpose of God, according to which he graciously regenerates, sanctifies, and saves sinners; that being perfectly consistent with the free agency of man, it comprehends all the means in connection with the end; that it is a most glorious display of God's sovereign goodness, being infinitely free, wise, holy, and unchangeable; that it utterly excludes boasting, and promotes humility, love, prayer, praise, trust in God, and active imitation of his free mercy; that it encourages the use of means in the highest degree; that it may be ascertained by its effects in all who truly believe the gospel; that it is the foundation of Christian assurance; and that to ascertain it with regard to ourselves demands and deserves the utmost diligence.

1. 2 Tim. 1:8-9; Eph. 1:3-14; 1 Pet. 1:1-2; Rom. 11:5-6; John 15:15; 1 John 4:19; Hos. 12:9

2. 2 Thess. 2:13-14; Acts 13:48; John 10:16; Matt. 20:16; Acts 15:14

3. Exod. 33:18-19; Matt. 20:15; Eph. 1:11; Rom. 9:23-24: Jer. 31:3; Rom. 11:28-29; James 1:17-18; 2 Tim. 1:9; Rom. 11:32-36

4. 1 Cor. 4:7; 1:26-31; Rom. 3:27; 4:16; Col. 3:12; 1 Cor. 3:5-7; 15:10; 1 Pet. 5:10; Acts 1:24; 1 Thess. 2:13; 1 Pet. 2:9; Luke 18:7; John 15:16; Eph. 1:16; 1 Thess. 2:12

5. 2 Tim. 2:10; 1 Cor. 9:22; Rom. 8:28-30; John 6:37-40; 2 Pet. 1:10

6. 1 Thess. 1:4-10

7. Rom. 8:28-30; Isa. 42:16; Rom. 11:29

8. 2 Pet. 1:10-11; Phil. 3:12; Heb. 6:11

X. OF SANCTIFICATION

We believe that Sanctification is the process by which, according to the will of God, we are made partakers of his holiness; that it is a progressive work; that it is begun in regeneration; and that it is carried on in the hearts of believers by the presence and power of the Holy Spirit, the Sealer and Comforter, in the continual use of the appointed means-especially the Word of God, self-examination, self-denial, watchfulness, and prayer.

1. 1 Thess. 4:3; 5:23; 2 Cor. 7:1; 13:9; Eph. 1:4

2. Prov. 4:18; 2 Cor. 3:18; Heb. 6:1; 2 Pet. 1:5-8; Phil. 3:12-16

3. John 2:29; Rom. 8:5; John 3:6; Phil. 1:9-11; Eph. 1:13-14

4. Phil. 2:12-13; Eph. 4:11-12; 1 Pet. 2:2; 2 Pet. 3:18; 2 Cor. 13:5; Luke 11:35; 9:23; Matt. 26:41; Eph. 6:18; 4:30

XI. OF THE PERSEVERANCE OF SAINTS

We believe that such only are real believers as endure unto the end; that their persevering attachment to Christ is the grand mark which distinguishes them from superficial professors; that a special Providence watches over their welfare; and they are kept by the power of God through faith unto salvation.

1. John 8:31; 1 John 2:27-28; 3:9; 5:18

2. 1 John 2:19; John 13:18; Matt. 13:20-21; John 6:66-69; Job 17:9

3. Rom. 8:28; Matt. 6:30-33; Jer. 32:40; Psa. 121:3; 91:11-12

4. Phil. 1:6; 2:12-13; Jude 24-25; Heb. 1:14; 2 Kings 6:16; Heb. 13:5; 1 John 4:4

XII. OF THE HARMONY OF THE LAW AND THE GOSPEL

We believe that the Law of God is the eternal and unchangeable rule of his moral government; that it is holy, just, and good; and that the inability which the Scriptures ascribe to fallen men to fulfill its precepts arises entirely from their love of sin; to deliver them from which, and to restore them through a Mediator to unfeigned obedience to the holy Law, is one great end of the Gospel, and of the means of grace connected with the establishment of the visible Church.

1. Rom. 3:31; Matt. 5:17; Luke 16:17; Rom. 3:20; 4:15

2. Rom. 7:12, 7, 14, 22; Gal. 3:21; Psa. 119

3. Rom. 8:7-8; Josh. 24:19; Jer. 13:23; John 6:44; 5:44

4. Rom. 8:2, 4; 10:4; 1 Tim. 1:5; Heb. 8:10; Jude 20-21; Heb. 12:14; Matt. 16:17-18; 1 Cor. 12:28

XIII. OF A GOSPEL CHURCH

We believe that a visible Church of Christ is a congregation of baptized believers, associated by covenant in the faith and fellowship of the gospel; observing the ordinances of Christ; governed by his laws, and exercising the gifts, rights, and privileges invested in them by his Word; that its only scriptural officers are Bishops, or Pastors, and Deacons, whose qualifications, claims, and duties are defined in the Epistles to Timothy and Titus.

1. 1 Cor. 1:1-13; Matt. 18:17; Acts 5:11; 8:1; 11:31; 1 Cor. 4:17; 14:23; 3 John 9; 1 Tim. 3:5

2. Acts 2:41-42; 2 Cor. 8:5; Acts 2:47; 1 Cor. 5:12-13

3. 1 Cor. 11:2; 2 Thess. 3:6; Rom. 16:17-20; 1 Cor. 11:23; Matt. 18:15-20; 1 Cor. 5:6; 2 Cor. 2:7; 1 Cor. 4:17

4. Matt. 28:20; John 14:15; 15:12; 1 John 4:21; John 14:21; 1 Thess. 4.2; 2 John 6; Gal. 6:2; all the Epistles

71

5. Eph. 4:7; 1 Cor. 14:12; Phil. 1:27; 1 Cor. 12:14

6. Phil. 1:1; Acts 14:23; 15:22; 1 Tim. 3; Titus 1

XIV. OF BAPTISM AND THE LORD'S SUPPER

We believe that Christian Baptism is the immersion in water of a believer, into the name of the Father, and Son, and Holy Ghost; to show forth, in a solemn and beautiful emblem, our faith in the crucified, buried, and risen Savior, with its effect in our death to sin and resurrection to a new life; that it is prerequisite to the privileges of a Church relation; and to the Lord's Supper, in which the members of the Church, by the sacred use of bread and wine, are to commemorate together the dying love of Christ; preceded always by solemn self-examination.

1. Acts 8:36-39; Matt. 3:5-6; John 3:22-23; 4:1-2; Matt. 28:19; Mark 16:16; Acts 2:38; 8:12; 16:32-34; 18:8

2. Matt. 28:19; Acts 10:47-48; Gal. 3:27-28

3. Rom. 6:4; Col. 2:12; 1 Pet. 3:20-21; Acts 22:16

4. Acts 2:41-42; Matt. 28:19-20; Acts and Epistles

5. 1 Cor. 11:26; Matt. 26:26-29; Mark 14:22-25; Luke 22:14-20

6. 1 Cor. 11:28; 5:1, 8; 10:3-32; 11:17-32; John 6:26-71

XV. OF THE CHRISTIAN SABBATH

We believe that the first day of the week is the Lord's Day, or Christian Sabbath; and is to be kept sacred to religious purposes, by abstaining from all secular labor and sinful recreations; by the devout observance of all the means of grace, both private and public; and by preparation for that rest that remained for the people of God.

1. Acts 20:7; Gen. 2:3; Col. 2:16-17; Mark 2:27; John 20:19; 1 Cor. 16:1- 2

2. Exod. 20:8; Rev. 1:10; Psa. 118:24

3. Isa. 58:13-14; 56:2-8

4. Psa. 119:15

5. Heb. 10:24-25; Acts 11:26; 13:44; Lev. 19:30; Exod. 46:3; Luke 4:16; Acts 17:2, 3; Psa. 26:8; 87:3

6. Heb. 4:3-11

XVI. OF CIVIL GOVERNMENT

We believe that civil government is of divine appointment, for the interests and good order of human society; and that magistrates are to be prayed for, conscientiously honored and obeyed; except only in things opposed to the will of our Lord Jesus Christ who is the only Lord of the conscience, and the Prince of the kings of the earth.

1. Rom. 13:1-7; Deut. 16:18; 1 Sam. 23:3; Exod. 18:23; Jer.30:21

2. Matt. 22:21; Titus 3:1; 1 Pet. 2:13; 1 Tim. 2:1-8

3. Acts 5:29; Matt. 10:28; Dan. 3:15-18; 6:7-10; Acts 4:18-20

4. Matt. 23:10; Rom. 14:4; Rev. 19:16; Psa. 72:11; Psa. 2; Rom. 14:9-13

XVII. OF THE RIGHTEOUS AND THE WICKED

We believe that there is a radical and essential difference between the righteous and the wicked;

that such only as through faith are justified in the name of the Lord Jesus, and sanctified by the Spirit of our God, are truly righteous in his esteem; while all such as continue in impenitence and unbelief are in his sight wicked, and under the curse; and this distinction holds among men both in and after death.

1. Mal. 3:18; Prov. 12:26; Isa. 5:20; Gen. 18:23; Jer. 15:19; Acts 10:34- 35; Rom. 6:16

2. Rom. 1:17; 7:6; 1 John 2:29; 3:7; Rom. 6:18, 22; 1 Cor. 11:32; Prov. 11:31; 1 Pet. 4:17-18

3. 1 John 5:19; Gal. 3:10; John 3:36; Isa. 57:21; Psa. 10:4; Isa 55:6-7

4. Prov. 14:32; Luke 16:25; John 8:21-24; Prov. 10:24; Luke 12:4-5; 9:23- 26; John 12:25-26; Eccl. 3:17; Matt. 7:13-14

XVIII. OF THE WORLD TO COME

We believe that the end of the world is approaching; that at the last day Christ will descend from heaven, and raise the dead from the grave to final retribution; that a solemn separation will then take place; that the wicked will be adjudged to endless punishment, and the righteous to endless joy; and that this judgment will fix forever the final state of men in heaven or hell, on principles of righteousness.

1. 1 Pet. 4:7; 1 Cor. 7:29-31; Heb. 1:10-12; Matt. 24:35; 1 John 2:17; Matt. 28:20; 13:39-40; 2 Pet. 3:3-13

2. Acts 1:11; Rev. 1:7; Heb. 9:28; Acts 3:21; 1 Thess. 4:13-18; 5:1-11.

3. Acts 24:15; 1 Cor. 15:12-59; Luke 14:14; Dan. 12:2; John 5:28-29; 6:40; 11:25-26; 2 Tim. 1:10; Acts 10:42

4. Matt. 13:49, 37-43; 24:30-31; 25:31-33

5. Matt. 25:35-41; Rev. 22:11; 1 Cor. 6:9-10; Mark 9:43-48; 2 Pet. 2:9; Jude 7; Phil. 3:19; Rom. 6:32; 2 Cor. 5:10-11; John 4:36; 2 Cor. 4:18

6. Rom. 3:5-6; 2 Thess. 1:6-12; Heb. 6:1-2; 1 Cor. 4:5; Acts 17:31; Rom. 2:2-16; Rev. 20:11-12; 1 John 2:28; 4:17

Tier I – Systematic Theology

According to "Systematic Theology: An introduction to Biblical Doctrine", Systematic theology is any study that answers the question, "What does the whole Bible teach us today?" about any given topic.[2]

There are anywhere between seven and twelve general topics that are organized to address different facets of the person and work of the Lord, the nature of man, and the like. Some are listed & explained below and come from Tabletalkmagazine.com.

- **Theology Proper** – This category considers God Himself, and it considers the nature of God, the names of God, the attributes of God, the works of God in creation and providence, and more.
- **Bibliology** – This category looks at the Book God has given us – The Bible… His focus is on the book of Scripture. It addresses issues such as the inspiration, authority, inerrancy, sufficiency, infallibility, and canon of Scripture.

---

[2] Wayne Grudem, "Systematic Theology: An introduction to Biblical Doctrine", (Grand Rapids, MI: Zondervan, 1995), p.21

- **Angelology** – These deal with the nature and works of angels.
- **Demonology** – These deal with the nature and works of demons.
- **Anthropology** – anthropology concerns the doctrine of man. When theologians discuss anthropology, they look at biblical teachings such as what it means to bear God's image, human nature as a body-soul duality, the vocations of men and women, true masculinity and femininity, and other topics.
- **Hamartiology** – deals with the doctrine of sin. The name for this topic comes for the Greek word for sin, hamartia, and looks at man as a sinner and the impact of sin on human nature. Therefore, hamartiology considers the fall of humanity, the nature and extend of sin, the impact of sin on human beings and the rest of creation, what sin and sinners deserve at the hands of our perfectly righteous God, and so on.
- **Christology** – includes the identity of Christ, who is the one divine person of the Son of God in whom are perfectly united the divine nature and human nature without confusion, division, change, or separation. In dealing with the person of Christ, Christology also usually answers various heresies related to

person of the Savior. In addition to the personhood of Jesus, Christology studies the work of Christ. Here we examine the threefold office of Christ as our Prophet, Priest, and King. In considering this threefold office, we also look at the incarnation of Christ; the active and passive obedience of Christ; the nature of the atonement and what it accomplished; and the exaltation of Christ in His resurrection, ascension, session (being seated at God's right hand), and return to judge the living and the dead.

- **Pneumatology** – Pneumatology examines what the Bible says about the person and work of the Holy Spirit. Here we study the deity of the Spirit, the procession of the Spirit from the Father and the Son, the gifts of the Spirit, the presence and work of the Spirit before and after the coming of Christ, and other important subjects. Pneumatology can be studied on its own, but sometimes theologians combine it with the work of soteriology.

- **Soteriology** – In soteriology, we seek to understand what God has done for us in the great work of redemption... the study of our salvation extends from eternity past and

God's covenant of redemption and election of His people to the completion of their salvation in their glorification. So, soteriology also examines regeneration, the outer and inner calls of the gospel, repentance, the nature of saving faith, justification, adoption, and sanctification. A study of the various covenants that God has made with human beings can also be studied here, but covenant theology can also be considered under another facet such as anthropology.

- **Ecclesiology** – This is the heading under which we study the doctrine of the church. Ecclesiology focuses on the church's unity, holiness, Apostolicity, and catholicity. It also considers how Jesus has organized His church, looking at the church's offices and structures. While dealing with the nature of the church, ecclesiology also looks at the marks of the church; the sound preaching of the Word, the right administration of the sacraments, and the proper exercise of church discipline.

- **Eschatology** – Eschatology deals with last things. The name of the category comes the Greek word for "last" or "ultimate". Eschatology considers personal eschatology

– what happens to individuals at the end, such as the nature of life after death, the intermediate state (the dwelling place and condition – people who die before Christ returns), and the resurrection of the body. Eschatology also considers topics such as the millennial reign of Christ, the antichrist, the sequence of events in the end times, and more.[3]

[3] Editorial, "Loci of Systematic Theology", TableTalk, March 2025

Tier I – Biblical Study

"Study to shew thyself approved of God, a workman that needeth not to be ashamed, rightly dividing the word of truth" – 2 Timothy 2:15

Preparation ("I will meditate in thy precepts, and have respect unto thy ways" -Psalm 119:15)

Effective Bible study begins with proper heart posture. In order to read and interpret the Bible properly, there must be an unquestionable belief in the Bible's inerrancy and infallibility. It is a collection of sixty-six books compiled over 2,000 years by 40 authors from 3 continents and varied walks of life, and using three languages and different genres. Yet there is an unfolding progressive narrative that remains unified. This is compelling evidence that the contents of the Bible came from one mind. The Scriptures tell us in 2 Peter that "prophecy never had its origin in the human will, but prophets, though human, spoke from God as they were carried along by the Holy Spirit" (NIV). When there is a belief in the truth of God's Word, teaching what it says (and ONLY what it says) becomes your primary goal.

Observation

The following steps are taken from "How to study the Bible" by Richard Mayhue:

Observe singularly – Do not look at any book other than the Bible. Put God's Book in a place all of its own.

Observe thoroughly – Start with the reminder that you will never see it all at one study… purpose to see as much as you can. Observe both the content and the context.

Observe systematically – Martin Luther studied the Bible as one who gathered apples. 'First, I shake the whole tree, so that the ripest may fall. Then I climb the tree and shake each limb, and then each branch and then each twig, and then I look under each leaf.'

Observe intimately – Look at it with the realization you are reading a message from the heavenly Father to you His spiritual child. It is like a letter from home while you are far away. [4]

---

[4] Richard Mayhue, "How to Read the Bible", (Great Britian: Christian Focus Publications, 2021), p.62-63.

Interpretation

When approaching the interpretation of Scripture, it is my belief that we must do so in the same manner we use when observing it… by using a literal approach based on the book's genre. The Torah (first 5 books of the Bible) and other historical books should be interpreted in a literal, or grammatical-historical fashion, while books of poetry, prophetic, and apocalyptic books should be interpreted symbolically based on culture of the time in which they were written. While we must rely on the Holy Spirit for illumination and the Bible is considered a supernatural book, it is a book, and should be interpreted in much the same manner we would any other source of information.

According to Charles Ryrie, there are three reasons to interpret the Bible in a literal, or grammatical-historical fashion:

1. If language is the creation of God for the purpose of conveying His message, then a theist must view that language as sufficient in scope and normative in use to accomplish that purpose for which God originated it.
2. The prophecies in the Old Testament concerning the first coming of Christ – His birth, His rearing, His ministry, His death, His

resurrection – were all fulfilled literally. That argues strongly for the literal method.

3. If one does not use the plain, normal, or literal method of interpretation, all objectivity is lost.[5]

I cannot stress the importance of the last point by Ryrie. If the Bible is to be interpreted in any other way, then no standard for interpretation exists, and the truth of the Bible is reduced to the opinions and narrative of the interpreter.

The most important thing to remember when interpreting the Scripture is context. Keep in mind that, while it was the Holy Spirit that guided men as they wrote the Bible, it was written in their language, for their culture in their day. In order to "rightly divide the Word of Truth" according to 2 Timothy 2:15, we must first determine what the original author was trying to say. Once we have done that, we can lift up, or exegete, the principals that God has laid before us in the text. Pastor Jim King, a professor at Carver Baptist Bible College, Institute & Theological Seminary, presents the following information at the beginning of every course, and it remains an immensely powerful tool.

---

[5] Charles C. Ryrie, "Dispensationalism: Revised & Expanded", (Chicago, IL: Moody Publishers, 2007), p. 92.

In the information he presents, Pastor King speaks of The Word of God as our foundation, with four contextual interpretations that serve as pillars for rightly dividing the Word of Truth. Those pillars are as follows:

Literal context – Taking God's Word literally where it is clearly intended to be taken literally and figuratively when it is clearly intended to be taken figuratively.

Grammatical context – Looking into the original language(s) of the text for clarification of word meanings.

Historical context – Looking into the history surrounding Biblical events. Understanding what was going on in the culture and the community during any given writing can shed important light on the text.

Written context – Looking at each word, sentence, verse, chapter, and book in context, which simply means "that which surrounds." Everything in life happens in a context – the circumstances, decisions, conversations, and outside influences. If we do not consider surrounding verses and chapters, we can come to unbiblical and even spiritually dangerous conclusions.

If we fail in any of these, then we cannot properly divide the word of truth, for even if one of the contextual pillars falls, the entire structure of biblical interpretation cannot stand.[6]

Application

The Bible can certainly be taught without practically applying its principles, but it can be taught more authoritatively when we live them out. Once we mine the theological principles communicated in the passages of Scripture, we must learn to make it a habit to "wear" them in our lives. Here are the suggested steps to help us do so:

- List the principles in the passage.
- Discover how that principle fits with the whole of Scripture.
- Determine how we can live out those principles.
  - Observe how the principles in the text address the original situation.
  - Discover a parallel situation in a contemporary context.

---

[6] Jim King (Pastor, Lee's Summit Bible Church in Lee's Summit, MO), August 17th, 2021.

      o Make the application specific - what specific ways can the principles apply?[7]

An *intimate* knowledge of Scripture becomes much more powerful than just *surface* knowledge. The difference becomes apparent when imparting it to someone else. When Jesus taught, Mark 1:22 says, "And they were astonished at His doctrine: for He taught them as one that had authority, and not as the scribes."

Applying the Scripture not only affords us the wisdom to offer life-changing instruction to someone else, but it also changes us.

The following worksheet can be used to teach the process and assess the level of proficiency in the candidate's ability to interpret Scripture in its context.

Bible Study Worksheet[8]

---

[7] J. Scott Duvall and J. Daniel Hays, "Grasping God's Word: A Hand-on approach to Reading, Interpreting, and Applying the Bible", (Grand Rapids, MI: Zondervan, 2012), p. 238-241.
[8] Mayhue, p. 82

(From Richard Mayhue's "How to Study the Bible")

Text: _____

Date: _____

1. Affirmation: God's Word is inerrant and infallible. I can believe it all and depend on it totally.
2. Preparation: I am studying to be approved by God, not ashamed before Him, because I cut the Word of Truth straight.
   In dealing with my sin, Jesus Christ is my intercessor through whom I can restore pure fellowship with God. The Holy Spirit is my divine illuminator. My Teacher and Guide.

What does the text say?

Observation:

What does the text mean by what it says?

Investigation:

Interpretation:

What else does the Bible say about this text?

Correlation:

How does this text apply to me?

Personalization:

How has this text impacted my life?

Appropriation:

With whom can I share what I have learned?
Proclamation:

Tier I – Apologetics

I believe that there should be some foundation that allows our church leaders to defend the faith that we say that we believe. 1 Peter 3:14b -15 says, "And do not be afraid of their threats, nor be troubled. But sanctify the Lord God in your hearts, and always be ready to give a defense to everyone who asks you a reason for the hope that is in you with meekness and fear (gentleness and respect)." The word 'defense' in this answer is the Greek word *apologia*, which means to make a reasoned statement or argument. Apologetics is not just defense, but offense, the positive task of constructing a case for Christianity that shows itself applicable in every culture, as well as being the only (and best) alternative to the world's philosophical and theological systems to thought. We would also do well to remember that our goal is not to win arguments, but to win souls.

In that vein, there are two principles of logic and knowledge I would like us to keep in mind when defending the faith.

- If something is true, the opposite of it is false. This is called the Law of Noncontradiction. Contradiction propositions cannot be both true and untrue at the same time in the same sense. An example would be, "The house is white and the house is not white."

  When applying this in a discussion with someone else, listening is particularly important. The key is discerning what someone is saying to be true, then comparing it to what is factually, and objectively true. For example, if someone says, "I always lie," we see a contradiction which would make this a false statement. Someone makes an assertion that they never tell the truth. If it is indeed true, then that makes the statement contradictory.

Even if it is a lie, then that means that person actually, at least sometimes, tells the truth. Ultimately, statements like these tend to collapse on themselves.

- Every effect must have a cause. This is called the Law of Causality. It is important to understand that this different from 'everything has a cause', because God is who we would call 'The First Cause'. He is not the effect because He has been ever Existent. This is effective for those who say the universe was caused by a Big Bang, because it begs the question, "What caused the Big Bang?" The Law of Causality is also the foundation for all sciences. Great discoveries and subsequent inventions took place because someone said, "what caused this to happen?"

In conclusion, when defending the faith, we can often successfully debunk arguments that seek to invalidate the doctrine when we hold to Scripture and the Laws of Logic. More importantly, as stated before, our main focus should not be the winning arguments, but the winning of souls. Any discussion about the faith should be made with both dignity and respect.

Tier II – Preaching & Teaching

In common usage, the
terms *preaching* and *teaching* are often used
interchangeably. There is, however, a significant
difference between them. Each endeavor plays a
unique role in evangelism and the spiritual
maturation of believers. To fully appreciate the
difference between preaching and teaching, it is
helpful to examine the original Greek terms used in
the New Testament, explore scriptural references,
and understand how both preaching and teaching
serve the mission of the church.

The Greek word for "preaching" is *kēryssō*, which is
a public proclamation of biblical truth. In the New
Testament, the early church proclaimed the gospel
throughout the Roman Empire. This proclamation
was intended to stir sinners to repentance. For
instance, Jesus began His earthly ministry with the
following charge: "Repent, for the kingdom of
heaven is at hand" (Matthew 4:17, ESV).
Repentance, then, is the goal of preaching.

On the other hand, the Greek term for "teach"
is *didaskō*, which refers to systematically imparting
knowledge and instruction. In the New Testament,
teaching involves biblical exposition to edify the

body of Christ. A great example of this is found in Acts 2:42, which says, "They [the early church] devoted themselves to the apostles' teaching and the fellowship, to the breaking of bread and the prayers" (ESV). The apostles shared the same teachings they had received from Jesus during His earthly ministry and post-resurrection appearances.[9]

Of course, there are many instances within the context of your local church where preaching and teaching is beneficial. Ephesians 4:11 lists both as offices necessary for the maturity of the saints, the work of the ministry, and the edifying of the body of Christ.

Aside from developing and growing the saints and uplifting the ministry of the church, there are some other practical benefits from preaching and teaching. To the one who is doing the preaching, it is an excellent opportunity to develop your preaching "style." It also helps the preacher/teacher to express their ideas clearly, and, if there is any hesitancy regarding public

---

[9] "What is the difference between preaching and teaching?", n.p., http://www.gotquestions.org/difference-preaching-teaching.html (accessed July 21 (Got Questions, 2025) (Iorg, 2003) (Jr, 1977) (Jr, Basic Principle of Biblical Counseling, 1975) (Frazier, 2011) (Frazier, 2011) (Thomas, 2025), 2025).

speaking, preaching and teaching can help to quell that a bit.

There are myriad examples in Scripture that emphasize both the purpose of preaching and teaching and its importance. 2 Timothy 4:2 exhorts to "Preach the word; be instant in season, out of season; reprove, rebuke, exhort with all longsuffering and doctrine." In context, there will come a time (and likely already here) that people will not endure sound doctrine. In the face of that, it becomes more important that we 'rightly divide' the Word of Truth according to 2 Timothy 2:15. A more sobering reason for understanding of its importance is James 3:1. Not many of you should become teacher, my fellow believers, because you know that we who teach will be judged more strictly (NIV)."

The principal purpose for preaching and teaching can be found in Colossians 1:28. "He is the One we proclaim, admonishing and teaching everyone with all wisdom, that we may present everyone mature in Christ (NIV)." The goal, then, is to see that practically, according to Ephesians 4:11. Teaching's purpose can be seen in Matthew 28:19-20 when we involve ourselves in discipleship. "go ye therefore, and teach all nations, baptizing them in the name of the Father, and of the Son, and of the Holy Ghost. Teaching them to observe all things whatsoever I have commanded you: and, lo, I am with always, even unto the end of the world. Amen." The word 'teach' in verse nineteen means to disciple, or to instruct, while the word 'teaching' in verse 20 means to enroll in a school of learning. Teaching, then, is as necessary for growth as preaching is for salvation. The instruction found in 1 Timothy 4:13... "... give attendance to reading, to exhortation, to doctrine." ... should not be taken lightly.

Although it would seem par for the course, today's preaching necessitates a reminder that all preaching and teaching should be Christocentric, or centered on Jesus Christ. Jesus Himself stated, "...All power is given unto Me in heaven and in earth (Matthew 28:18)", and "...I am the Way, the Truth, and the Life: no man cometh unto the Father, but by Me (John 14:6)." On the road to Emmaus Christ spoke to men regarding what all the prophets have spoken. "And beginning at Moses and all the prophets, He expounded unto them in all the Scriptures the things concerning Himself (Luke 24:27)." This underlines the importance of keeping Christ (and no one else!) in the center of our preaching and teaching. It is in the name of Jesus that every knee should bow, of things in heaven, and things in earth, and things under the earth. And that every tongue should confess that Jesus Christ is Lord, to the glory of God the Father." He is the only way in which we can be saved according to Acts 4:12. "Neither is there salvation in any other; for there is none other name under heaven given among men, whereby we must be saved."

Again, it may seem obvious, but it is equally important that our preaching is Bibliocentric. If Christ is to be the center of our preaching, our teaching should be rooted in the Bible, since it reflects the heart and mind of God, and is written for us to show us how we should live. Romans 15:4 says, "For whatsoever things were written aforetime were written for our learning, that we through patience and comfort of the Scriptures might have hope." The use of extra-Biblical resources is great for underscoring the principles taught in Scriptures, but they should not be the primary source in which our teaching should be based. Books or resources which are heavily based in Scripture could be considered, but it is the Bible in which our teachings should be founded on. It is the Bible that has the ability to affect deep abiding change in the life of the individual, as it is God-breathed. 2 Timothy 3:16-17 says, "All Scripture is given by inspiration of God, and is profitable for doctrine, for reproof, for correction, for instruction in righteousness."

Finally, I would like to emphasize a few things. First, I want to re-iterate "rightly dividing the Word of Truth." In order to be able to accurately deliver the unadulterated Word of God, we must take seriously the responsibility of preaching and teaching. Secondly, while we must follow the leading of the Holy Spirit, we must not forget to be who we are. The demonstration of preaching and teaching becomes more effective when we refrain from practicing "styles" that imitate someone else. Be yourself, and God's power and influence will become much more evident, not only to you but to your audience. The following has been credited to both Alistair Begg and W. H. Griffith Thomas, and it is recommended when preparing for, and operating in, the area of preaching and teaching:

THINK YOURSELF EMPTY

READ YOURSELF FULL

WRITE YOURSELF CLEAR

PRAY YOURSELF HOT

BE YOURSELF, BUT DON'T PREACH
YOURSELF

Tier II – Ministry Skills Development

Once the gift assessment has been completed by the candidate, careful planning should take place in developing that gift to determine what specific role the associate minister is to play. While there would be general functions such as pulpit conducting, or filling in while the pastor is away, the associate minister should also be given the opportunity to serve according to his particular gifting. Below are suggested steps to help the associate minister develop his gifts:

- Once the gift has been determined, set achievable milestones, if possible (if counseling, place on a counseling track, etc.).
- Workshops, seminars, online courses focused on your area can be helpful.
- Have them study biblical examples of Biblical leadership.
- Help them find a mentor, if possible.
- Have them volunteer in the church or community to develop their skill.
- Ensure the candidate is consistent in their spiritual disciplines.
- Share what you have learned.
- Celebrate progress.

- Be open to pivoting or deepening your focus as God leads.

Remember, ministry is a lifelong journey – We all should keep learning, serving, and growing.

Tier II – Leadership/Administration

According to "The character of Leadership" by Jeff Iorg, leadership roles, positions, callings, or assignments are God's laboratories for leaders. God places us where we are (or may call us to a new place) so He can have the perfect laboratory for continuing to change us into the image of Jesus.[10] I believe this is an important mindset to have when in leadership, as it cements a focus on the task of leadership and disconnects us from an inward focused approach to it. Understanding we are being made to be more like Jesus (in whatever position God puts us in) reminds us that our efforts are for *His* purposes and not our own. With that in mind, Iorg gives us nine qualities that define good leaders. Those qualities are as follows:

---

[10] Jeff Iorg, "The Character of Leadership"(Nashville, TN: B & H Publishing Group, 2003), p.7-8.

1. **Integrity** – Living with honesty and consistency, even when no one is watching.
2. **Security** – Leading from a place of emotional and spiritual stability, not insecurity or fear.
3. **Purity** – Maintaining moral and ethical clarity, especially in private conduct.
4. **Humility** – Recognizing one's limitations and serving others without arrogance.
5. **Servanthood** – Prioritizing the needs of others and leading through service.
6. **Wisdom** – Applying knowledge with discernment and spiritual insight.
7. **Discipline** – Practicing self-control and perseverance in habits and decisions.
8. **Courage** – Facing challenges and opposition with boldness and faith.
9. **Passion** – Leading with heartfelt conviction and enthusiasm for the mission[11]

Having reviewed the qualifications of an elder, the ministerial candidate is probably exhibiting most, if not all these qualifications, but leadership and administration tend to be a continual and evolving position especially when the needs of the local church continue to change. The following is

---

[11] Iorg, summary of Table of Contents

suggested curriculum designed to either cultivate or enhance the nine leadership qualities outlined in Jeff Iorg's framework:

Duration: 9 Weeks

Format: Weekly sessions for individual or group study

Focus: Cultivating Christlike leadership through Scripture, spiritual practices, and visual metaphors of transformation

■ Weekly Session Format

Each week includes:

- **Scripture Exploration**
- **Biblical Case Study**
- **Spiritual Practice**
- **Visual Metaphor Reflection**
- **Creative/Relational Application**

Week 1: Integrity

Scripture: Daniel 1–6

Case Study: Daniel's refusal to compromise.

Practice: Confession and journaling

Visual Metaphor: *Kintsugi* – Brokenness restored with gold.

Activity: Create a collage of personal failures and redemptive moments using gold accents

Week 2: Security

Scripture: Psalm 91; Romans 8

Case Study: David's trust in God during exile

Practice: Breath prayer and meditation on identity in Christ

Visual Metaphor: *Anchor* – Stability in storms

Activity: Draw or sculpt an anchor with embedded affirmations

Week 3: Purity

Scripture: Psalm 51; Matthew 5:8

Case Study: David's repentance

Practice: Guided confession and renewal ritual

Visual Metaphor: *Refining fire* – Gold purified through heat.

Activity: Burn symbolic "impurities" written on paper, then write a prayer of renewal

Week 4: Wisdom

Scripture: Proverbs 3; James 3

Case Study: Solomon's discernment

Practice: Lectio Divina on Proverbs

Visual Metaphor: *Tree with deep roots* – Grounded and fruitful

Activity: Map out a "wisdom tree" with roots (sources of wisdom) and branches (actions)

Week 5: Courage

Scripture: Joshua 1; Esther 4

Case Study: Esther's boldness

Practice: Silence and declaration (naming fears, speaking truth)

Visual Metaphor: *Molting* – Shedding old skin to grow.

Activity: Create a layered art piece showing what's being shed and what's emerging.

Week 6: Passion

Scripture: Romans 12; John 2:13–17

Case Study: Jesus cleansing the temple.

Practice: Fasting and vision-casting

Visual Metaphor: *Flame* – Controlled fire that energizes.

Activity: Paint or write about what "sets your heart on fire" for God's mission

Week 7: Humility

Scripture: Philippians 2; John 13

Case Study: Jesus washing feet.

Practice: Foot-washing or service project

Visual Metaphor: *Empty vessel* – Ready to be filled.

Activity: Create a clay or paper vessel and write prayers of surrender inside

Week 8: Servanthood

Scripture: Mark 10:42–45; Luke 10

Case Study: The Good Samaritan

Practice: Acts of hidden service **Visual Metaphor**: *Towel and basin* – Tools of quiet service

Activity: Write anonymous encouragement or serve someone without recognition

Week 9: Discipline

Scripture: Hebrews 12; 1 Corinthians 9

Case Study: Paul's self-control

Practice: Rule of life creation

Visual Metaphor: *Vineyard trellis* – Structure that enables growth.

Activity: Design a personal "trellis" with spiritual habits and boundaries

Tier II – Counseling

Because of the mysterious nature of the human psyche, my first suggestion is to have the ministerial candidate go to school to take counseling classes. It is also because of the nature of the psyche that I would strongly suggest those classes are Biblically based counseling classes. No one is as familiar with the nature of man than God, who created him. If there is anyone who can navigate the complexities of the mind and heart, it is the Lord. With that being said, Lawrence J Crabb Jr, author of "Effective Biblical Counseling", introduces an alternative method to those who seek counseling for the purposes of seeking happiness or fulfillment: "It seems to me that a seriously neglected truth in most Christian counseling efforts is this: the basic biblical reason for wanting to solve your personal problem should be that you want to enter into a deeper relationship with God, to more effectively please Him through praise and worship."[12] His belief was that "...the most basic problem of every human being is his separation from God, a gulf made necessary by the fact that God is holy and we are not."[13]

Of course, there can be natural or physical causes that could be the root of some dysfunction and this is why some formal counseling education is necessary (or, at the very least, available referrals to licensed counselors when recognized).

Please keep in mind that, because all people have been created in the image of God, they all have should be treated as having worth, dignity, and value. All of us have different experiences, come from different backgrounds, and have different perspectives on things as a result. In light of those differences, it is paramount to spend as much time

---

[12] Lawrence J Crabb Jr, "Effective Biblical Counseling" (Grand Rapids, MI: Zondervan, 1977), p.21
[13] Lawrence J Crabb Jr, "Basic Principle of Biblical Counseling" (Grand Rapids, MI: Zondervan, 1975), p.17

as necessary to understand those we counsel and
ensure that counsel is rooted in the Word of God,
and any counsel that is otherwise delivered will not
stand.

Tier II – Evangelism/Outreach

The following is an excerpt from "Strategies for Developing an Effective Evangelism Program" by Pastor Emeritus Jesse Frazier (Ebenezer Missionary Baptist Church), originally presented at the Williams Bible Conference at Carver Baptist Theological Seminary March 16-18, 2011.

One of the most difficult tasks in the church in the 21st century is to develop and maintain a viable evangelism program. It is terribly difficult to pin down any one reason why pastors find it hard to organize, to staff and to maintain this elusive arm of ministry. This problem pricks many of our hearts because we know God has ordained evangelism as the means of harvesting the precious fruit of the earth, "the souls of men." There is no question about the marching orders of the church. Matthew 28: 18-20; Acts 1:8; 2 Corinthians 5:17-6:1 and Ephesians 2:8-10 are just a few of the verses we need to consider when we think about what the Lord's will is for this dying world, and what the church should be doing to get the work done. I know it is easier said than done, but the church has not been given a task that is impossible for it to achieve. The Lord has not only gifted the church to do soul winning but empowered and compelled Her to do it. One of the major problems I've observed is that a paradigm shift has taken place in the church, in general, that has led to the lack of trained evangelist in the field in particular. The emphasis for soul-winning has shifted from the pew to the pulpit and because of that we, to some degree, have lost our way. My statements here should not be taken as an indictment of any pastor or ministry, but as it is, general information. I believe the shift spawned in the pit of

hell because, as a result of it we have lost much of our effectiveness at reaching souls. Pulpits were never ordained by God to evangelize, but to teach, train, nurture and help bring to maturity the pew member so that they could evangelize, Eph. 4:11-12. We've gone away from the biblical prescription of how it should be done and we have suffered for it. For some reason, the average pew member believes it is the pastor's job to seek and save that which is lost. And unless that view is changed, we will continue to have the problem that pervades the church today. Harnessing the power of the pew is no small feat, but is highly doable and deeply rewarding. When I first read Acts chapter 8:1-4 my joy went through the roof because I saw the general membership of the church scattered abroad and the text says they went everywhere preaching the word. We have to pay close attention to the narrative because it states that the apostles stayed at Jerusalem. If the apostles (leaders) (pulpit servants) stayed at Jerusalem, who was it that went everywhere preaching the word? Ah! You got it, the pew member. Beloved, if we are going to maximize the opportunities given to us by God to evangelize the world, we will need to reclaim the biblical prescription for getting it done. We will have to go back to the point of preparing each born again believer to be a witness, and a light that's thoroughly equipped to proclaim the Resurrected Savior, Jesus the Christ the Son of the Living God. Two final thoughts before we talk about how we can go back and reclaim the biblical prescription for preparing the saints to serve. First, many of us have been heirs to a broken system relative to evangelism. We learned from our pastors what was deemed evangelism and they learned from their pastors and leaders before them and so on. Consequently, this ineffective way of going about doing evangelism has been perpetuated from generation to generation. The question is when we know better, will we do better? I trust that we will. Secondly, Dr. Thomas P. Johnston stated in his book The Theology of Evangelism, that there are 72 different ways to do evangelism delineated into 17 different categories, giving us a wide range of methodologies and ideas for soul winning. Because there are so many ways to go about soul winning, we can use methodologies that best fit our particular congregations and overall ministry thrust. The message should never change but the methods must. Listed below are some practical steps to take into consideration when you move toward establishing an effective evangelism ministry in your fellowship.

1. Cast the evangelism vision using the biblical model.
   a. Teach a series on biblical evangelism.
   b. Share with the congregation what God expects of them.
   c. Review with them the first century model of soul-winning.

2. Cultivate a soul-winning environment in your fellowship.
   a. Start sharing in new membership class and discipleship training the reasons why God chose them.
   b. Use your Sunday school class as an evangelistic tool.

c. Evangelism should be woven into the fabric of the fellowship.

3. Move your training beyond the classroom to the field.

   a. There's only so much to be learned in the classroom. Your new soul-winners need real world experience.

   b. Arm them with salvation scripture references.

   c. Have them internalize the two questions of assurance. *

4. Partner new workers with seasoned soul-winners.

   a. One of the greatest ways to get new soul-winners seasoned is by teaming them up with veteran soul-winners. They will gain a wealth of knowledge by standing and observing others lead people to Christ.

   b. Gradually allow them an opportunity to share the Gospel.

5. Diversify your methodologies for the sake of all involved.

   a. Use invitational evangelism as a means of getting the general congregation involved.

   b. Use vacation bible school and Sunday school as a means of getting your teaching staff involved in evangelism.

   c. Use your visitation team and phone calling committee as means of evangelizing your visitors.

   d. Use your street and outreach team as a second equipping level for itinerant evangelist and anyone else willing to take the next step.

6. Get your prayer ministry and the general fellowship involved in prayer continually for the souls of men.

   a. God is the true evangelist; we are partnering with Him.

   b. Pray for the Lord to lead, guide and empower each effort, regardless of

the methodology being used at the
time.

c. Pray with great confidence because
you are moving in the absolute will of
God. Soul-winning is His will!

Above all else be patient because training soul-
winners is a slow process. Moving the general
fellowship toward a soul-winning mindset is a
monumental task but it will pay great dividends as
you start to see progress and hear the praise
reports. Remember when casting your vision for
shifting to a soul-winners mindset, share with your
leadership team first. Then share with all of your
auxiliary team leaders and on to the general
congregation. As you start to weave into the fabric
of the fellowship the soul-winners philosophy, the
transition will be smoother and the involvement
from the general pew member greater. I pray God's
choice blessings upon your every effort.[14]

---

[14] Jesse Frazier, "Strategies for Developing an Effective
Evangelism Program", Williams Bible Conference, Kansas
City, MO, March 16-18, 2011.

*" If you died today and God asked you 'why should I let you into My heaven', what would you tell Him?" or "If you died today, do you know where you would spend eternity?"

Although there are myriads of ways to present the gospel, below are passages in the Book of Romans that can help lead someone to Christ (called the Roman Road, KJV).

Romans 3:10 and Romans 3:23 informs us of our standing before God – sinners in need of grace.

Romans 6:23a advises us of the consequence of our standing as sinners – eternal death.

Romans 5:8 describes the proactive nature of God's love toward us.

Romans 6:23b helps us to understand the free gift of Jesus as payment for our sin. John 3:16 can also be introduced here.

Romans 10:8-10 details how someone can be saved from the penalty of sin.

Romans 10:13 simplifies the process of salvation.

Tier II – Membership Care

Membership Care is a vital component of those who are in a leadership position as it personifies what we ought to be to one another as followers of Christ. James 1:27 says, "Pure religion and undefiled before God and the Father is this, to visit the fatherless and widows in their affliction, and to keep himself unspotted from the world." It brings ministry to a personal level, and has the ability to encourage both the layperson and those in leadership. The following has been contributed by Pastor Scott Thomas of Starlight Missionary Baptist Church of Kansas City, Missouri and outlines an excellent process as it relates to Member Care:

"I was sick, and you looked after me." Matthew 25:36

Visiting someone in the hospital is a great ministry in the church. Through visitation people are encouraged and given hope for their sickness, injuries, and mental state. Your visit is a reminder to a patient of God's love demonstrated through His church. Furthermore, visiting the sick can lead to opportunities that may allow you to share the Gospel with their unbelieving family members and extend your ministry beyond the hospital visit. You are an ambassador for Christ, for your church, and your pastor every time you make a hospital visit. Here are some guidelines to help as you make hospital visits:

Before the Visit:

Get as much information as possible about the patient by:

> - Attempting to find out the diagnosis and condition of the patient.
> - Calling to make sure the patient is still in the hospital. Make sure they can receive visitors or would like a visit.
> - Refer to the church directory if necessary for more information about the member.
> - Pray and ask for God's guidance and direction.
> - Consider a proper scripture passage for the situation.

During the Visit:

When you arrive at the patient's room, remember to:

> - Knock before entering the room.
> - Show no shock by what you see.
> - Identify who you are and church affiliation if it is unknown.

- Do not sit on the patient's bed.
- Keep advice to a minimum. Do more listening and allow the person to vent their grief if needed.
- Resist the temptation to say, "Don't cry," or "You've got to hold yourself together".
- Allow the conversation to be directed by the patient.
- Be as encouraging as possible without giving a false prognosis.
- Avoid talking about yourself and your problems.
- Do not be insulted by the patient's words or attitudes.
- Do not out diagnose the doctor or offer false optimism.
- Respect other patients and their guests.
- Be wise about the length of time spent during the visit. A good rule is to make your visit brief and not stay too long. Remember to use good discernment.
- Let your prayer and scripture be proper for the occasion.
- Be prepared to share the Gospel.
- If visiting more than one person, do not carry stirred emotions from visit to visit.

After The Visit

➢ Follow up a phone call to find out the person's condition.
➢ Provide a follow-up visit if necessary.
➢ Use the same procedure for future visits.

Remember, visitation is a ministry. It is a way to serve others and encourage them when they are sick. We must take it seriously because it is possible that the act of kindness can lead someone to Christ. [15]

---

[15] Scott Thomas (Pastor of Starlight Missionary Baptist Church), email message to author, September 2, 2025.

It is my prayer that the information provided would be of some assistance to both the pastor and the man who God has called to be his associate. I want to be clear this book is not an absolute in training or readiness in ministry, but a guideline. There are some things the local pastor may not agree with exactly, and others which you as the pastor should feel free to tweak or adjust based on the needs of your local body. I also want to remind us that the book is not to be used to determine if a candidate has received a call, although the pastor could decide that the candidate may not be ready at the time. As a bit of an aside, many who have received God's call…whether deacon, minister, pastor, or usher… may already be moving in that capacity without the title. The process of aiding the associate in his call should not be limited by a timeline. Ultimately, we are all on a journey of a lifetime of learning. It is the decision of the pastor, as God is directing him, to determine when the associate minister becomes licensed or ordained. It is my fervent hope that the guidebook could be instrumental part of this important process.

Other Helpful information

Because this book began as an assistant to the pastor, I thought another thing that could be of assistance would be a resource that could aid in assimilating new members to the membership. I believe that Pastor Scott Thomas has put together an outstanding plan that could do just that. With his permission, I have added that plan here. I believe it to be a great help in lessening those instances in which those who become new members only stay for a short time, but then are gone again. It has been helpful to me, as I have instituted many of the suggestions and we have a higher percentage of member retention than the norm. I pray it is of a great benefit to the pastor.

Establishing An Assimilation Plan For Your Church

If the Lord decided to suddenly send one hundred people to your church, what would you do? Although the Lord may not send one hundred members to your church at once, He may send them in small increments. Yet the question remains, How would you help the people he sends become involved and a part of your church? An assimilation plan is a great start.

I.   What is an assimilation plan?
It is a plan to help new Christians and new members become a part of and learn the Christian culture so they will become mature followers of Christ. Before a person became a Christian they were "dead in trespasses and sins" and "walked according to the course of this world", Ephesians 2:1 – 2. When they were regenerated, the Holy Spirit baptized them by immersing them into the Body of Christ making them one with Christ, John 4:10; 1 Corinthians 12:13. This spiritual baptism must now be made manifest through a local church. They must be unified with a local body of believers where they can drink living water through worship, growth, fellowship, service, and evangelism, so they will become mature in Christ, Ephesians 4:11 – 13. If not, they are in danger of reverting to confusion, carnality, deformity, and disconnection. To help prevent this from happening, churches need an assimilation plan. It is an organized approach to helping new converts and other Christians who join a church learn to be devoted to Christ and grow to maturity.

II. What's involved in an assimilation plan?

There are three main functions involved in assimilation:

Firstly, it should provide information to members about your church. The information will help them understand what is involved in being a church member. Here is some information that can be shared:

> - **The goals of the church** – Vision and Mission of the church.
> - **Membership objectives** – What the church would like to see accomplished in the members.
> - **Membership benefits** – What the members can expect from the Church
> - **Members duties and responsibilities** – What the church can expect from members.
> - **Next steps** – What their next steps will be.

Secondly, it should provide beginner's training. The training will help with basic Christian development. It can involve:

> - **Doctrinal class** – teaching in the fundamentals of the faith.

- ➢ **Church government class** – teaching in the operations and government of your church
- ➢ **Basic duties class** – teaching them about their duties and responsibilities to the church.
- ➢ **Spiritual Gifts Assessment** – a survey to help them discover their Spiritual Gift(s).
- ➢ **Training about purchasing a Bible.** Teach members to use the translation your church uses for preaching and teaching. You can also help them to determine what type of (study) Bible to purchase.
- ➢ **Training in where and in what ways they can serve.** They can also be introduced to ministry leaders or events leaders.

Thirdly, it should provide help with placement. The placement should involve areas of continuing Christian fellowship, instruction, and service.

- ➢ They should be directed to a Sunday School, Discipleship class, or small groups, whichever your church offers.
- ➢ They should be assisted with being placed in a ministry where they can serve.
- ➢ They should be assisted with being placed in a ministry or with mentors for fellowship.
- ➢ They should be encouraged to bring others with them to church.

During the time of assimilation, new members need shepherding. The assimilation person should make regular contacts via phone, text, or in person. They should help by answering questions, providing words of encouragement, and praying with them.

III.   What are the stages of an assimilation plan?

Now that we have defined an assimilation plan, it's functions, what stages are involved? There are two stages to the assimilation process. There is the Initial Stage and the Placement Stage.

Initial Stage

The initial stage involves steps to help them become acquainted with the church. You will provide them with:

> **Membership orientation.** Membership orientation will allow you to explain you're your church's vision, mission, expectations, and the next steps for ministry.
> **New Members Class.** This class can teach about your church's beliefs such as denomination beliefs, doctrinal beliefs, or form of church government.

- ➢ **Assistance with purchasing a Bible.**
- ➢ **Membership follow up.** Contacting members through letters, cards, emails, calls, or text messages.
- ➢ **Spiritual Gifts Assessment.** An assessment survey to help members discover their Spiritual Gift(s) and find a place to serve.
- ➢ **Graduation Certificate.**

Connection Stage

The Connection Stage helps them get involved and become a part of your church. You will help them:

- ➢ **Connect them to Ministries.** Areas of service for members to be involved in the work of the church.
- ➢ **Connect them to Sunday School.** Teaching and training for Christian growth and maturity.
- ➢ **Connect them to One-on-one discipleship.** One on one mentoring to help develop members.
- ➢ **Connect them to mentors Fellowship groups.** Groups for fellowship and learning.
- ➢ **Connect them to Community events or projects.** Outreach and evangelistic events and projects to reach others in our families and the community.

It doesn't take many people to get started. The size of your church and the pace of growth will determine the amount needed. It can take only one assimilation leader or guide to manage up to 10 people in the initial stage.

Conclusion

Establishing an assimilation plan is not an exact science. What works for some churches doesn't work for others. It takes hearing from the Lord God through prayer and discovering how he wants to direct your church. He has all wisdom and power, and you must ask Him for guidance about what ideas to use, and what fits with your church. Churches with an assimilation plan will produce members that are mature. They will be unified and purposeful because they have direction and know where they are going. These churches fulfill the Great Commission and bring glory to the Lord. However, churches without an assimilation plan will produce members that remain immature. They will become stagnant, ineffective, deformed. Their membership may eventually decline because people will not remain engaged. In a blog written by church researcher, Tony Morgan, he says one of the reasons churches are in decline is because of a ***"Failure to define a concise strategy to help newcomers become fully devoted followers of Christ"***.[16] This decline happens when the "back door" of the church is left opened. Leaving the "back door" open occurs when people who are members of a church, become dissatisfied because they don't have clear direction about expectations, growth, and involvement. Therefore, they leave and become a member somewhere else without informing anyone. They came through the "front door" by coming to the alter but leave through the "back door" by covertly disconnecting. Though we cannot keep every member, we can make attempts to close the back door. We can discover ways to help them with clear direction, so they become useful and get involved. An assimilation plan can help, and can is the place to start.

Bibliography

McIntosh, Gary L. *"Beyond The First Visit"*. Grand Rapids MI: Baker Books, 2007. Print.

---

[16] Works Cited: "5 Attributes of a Church in Decline". The Unstuck Group, July 15, 2010. Web. 19 February 2024.

McIntosh, Gary L. *"Biblical Church Growth"*. Grand Rapids MI: Baker Books, 2003. Print.

Rainer, Thom S. *"High Expectations"*. Nashville TN: B&H Publishing Group, 1999. Print

Bibliography

Editorial. (2025, March). Loci of Systematic Theology. *Tabletalk.*

Frazier, J. (2011). Strategies for Developing an Effective Evangelism Program. *Williams Bible Conference.* Kansas City.

Got Questions. (2025, July 21). *What is the difference between preaching and teaching?* Retrieved from GotQuestions.org: https://www.gotquestions.org/differenc-preaching-teaching.html

Grudem, W. (1995). *Systematic Theology: An Introduction to Biblical Doctrine.* Grand Rapids: Zondervan.

Hays, J. S. (2012). *Grasping God's Word: A Hands-on approach to Reading, Interpreting, and Applying the Bible.* Grand Rapids: Zondervan.

Iorg, J. (2003). *The Character of Leadership.* Nashville: B & H Publishing Group.

Jr, L. J. (1975). *Basic Principle of Biblical Counseling.* Grand Rapids: Zondervan.

Jr, L. J. (1977). *Effective Bible Counseling .* Grand Rapids: Zondervan.

King, J. (2021, August 17). Lee's Summit, MO.

Mayhue, R. (2021). *How to Read the Bible.* Great Britian: Christian Focus Publications.

Ryrie, C. C. (2007). *Dispensationalism: Revised and Expanded.* Chicago: Moody Publishers.

Thomas, S. (2025, September 2). Visitation Procedure. Kansas City, MO.

What are the essentials of the Christian Faith? (2025, August 1). Retrieved from GotQuestions.org: https://www.gotquestions.org/essentials-Christian-faith.htm